party cocktails

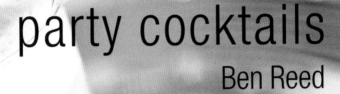

party cocktails

Ben Reed

photography by
William Lingwood

RYLAND
PETERS
& SMALL
LONDON NEW YORK

Designer Saskia Janssen
Editor Miriam Hyslop
Production Gavin Bradshaw
Art Director Gabriella Le Grazie
Publishing Director Alison Starling

First published in the United States in 2005
by Ryland Peters & Small, Inc.
519 Broadway, 5th Floor
New York, NY 10012
www.rylandpeters.com

10 9 8 7 6 5 4 3 2 1

Text © Ben Reed 2005
Design and photographs
© Ryland Peters & Small 2005

The recipes in this book have been previously published by
Ryland Peters & Small.

ISBN 1 84172 970 1

Printed in China.

contents

Next time you entertain at home why not offer something different on the libation front and serve some irresistible cocktails? With the tips and recipes in this book, you'll soon be serving cocktails with complete confidence.

First, position your bar so that your guests can see their drinks being prepared. Don't make the mistake of placing your bar in the corner, you need to be able to move around freely. Secondly, plan to serve just three or four cocktails—and stick to them (include at least one non-alcoholic cocktail). Have a drink ready to serve to your guests when they arrive. Once all your guests have a drink in hand, you can take some time over preparing more complicated cocktails.

If you assemble your drinks in advance, remember that ice will melt, cocktails will warm up and separate, and any carbonated drinks will lose their fizz. The most efficient way to prepare a shaken cocktail ahead is to pour the ingredients into the mixing glass without ice and leave it to one side. When you are ready to serve the cocktail, add the ice, shake it good and hard, and pour into your chosen glass.

All recipes in this book serve one. If you want to make more than one, say, French Martini (see page 16), multiply the ingredients by the number of cocktails—a shaker should hold three. For cocktails containing ice and sparkling drinks, such as the Mojito (see page 40), mix the rest of the ingredients in advance, and add the ice and fizz just before serving.

techniques

There are five basic ways of creating a cocktail: building, blending, shaking, stirring over ice, and muddling. Whichever method you are using, accurately measure the ingredients first to get that all-important balance of tastes right. If you would rather try guesswork just see how much practise it takes to get the quantity right to fill the glass exactly—I still have problems in that department!

The process of **building** a cocktail just requires adding the measured ingredients to the appropriate glass, with plenty of ice, and giving it a quick stir before serving. The **blending** method involves pouring all the ingredients into a blender, adding crushed ice, and flicking the switch. Using a shaker is the most enjoyable way to mix a cocktail, both for you and your guests. Add the ingredients to the shaker and fill it with ice. The **shaking** movement should be sharp and fairly assertive, but do remember to keep your hands on both parts of the shaker, or at least a finger on the cap. Drinks containing egg white, cream, and juices should be shaken for slightly longer than the usual ten seconds. **Stirring** is the best method when you want to retain the clarity and strength of the liquors. Manhattans, for example, are always stirred. Use an ice-filled mixing glass and stir carefully to avoid chipping the ice and diluting the drink. Frost your serving glasses by leaving them in the refrigerator for an hour before use. The **muddling** technique involves using the flat end of a barspoon or a muddler to mix or crush ingredients such as fruit or herbs and allow the flavors to be released gently.

To make **simple syrup**, place in a pan five cups of superfine sugar to four cups of water. Stir and dissolve the sugar until the liquid is clear. Let cool, and bottle it. Simple syrup can be kept in the refrigerator for a couple of weeks.

equipment

The first thing any aspiring bartender should acquire is a **measure** (jigger). Too many professional bartenders regard the jigger as a tool for the novice—their guesswork results in many delicate cocktails being ruined. The modern dual-measure jigger measures both 2 oz. and 1 oz. (a double and a single measure). The **shaker** is the second most important piece of equipment for a bartender. The **barspoon**, with its long spiralling handle, is useful for stirring drinks. The "wrong," flat end can be used for muddling or crushing herbs, etc. A **muddler**, a wooden pestle for mixing or crushing sugar cubes, limes, etc., and the **bartender's friend** for opening cans and removing corks and bottle caps, are also handy. A **mixing glass** with strainer is used for making drinks that are stirred, not shaken. Other useful accessories include an **ice bucket**, **ice tongs**, and a **juice squeezer**.

glasses

The traditional **martini glass** is a very familiar icon, with its open face and slim stem. The **cocktail glass** is similar to the martini glass but with a slightly rounded bowl. The **rocks** or **old fashioned glass** is a squat, straight-sided glass, which sits on a heavy base and feels comfortable in the hand. The **highball** and the **collins glasses** come in various sizes but they are all tall, slim glasses designed to keep a long drink fresh and cold. The small, sturdy **shot glass** is designed with one purpose: getting the drink from one's glass into one's mouth with minimal fuss. The **champagne flute** is perfect for keeping the sparkle in your champagne cocktails. It should be elegant and long-stemmed, with a narrow rim to enhance the delicacy of the drink.

vodka

classic martini

This is how I would make a "standard" martini for anyone who requested one. Stirring the cocktail is a more authentic method, and the original labor of love for any bartender.

a dash of vermouth (Noilly Prat or
   Martini Extra Dry)
2 ½ oz. well-chilled vodka or gin
olive or lemon twist, to garnish

Add both the ingredients to a mixing glass filled with ice, and stir. Strain into a frosted martini glass, and garnish with an olive or lemon twist.

pontberry martini

2 oz. vodka
2 ½ oz. cranberry juice
a large dash of crème de mure

This martini is a cinch to prepare since it involves no fresh fruit. Strong and sweet, it should appeal to a wide range of tastes.

Shake all the ingredients in a shaker filled with ice. Strain into a frosted martini glass and serve.

citrus martini

Another old favorite, this martini needs to be
shaken hard to take the edge off the lemon.
Try substituting lime for lemon for a slightly more
tart variation.

Add all the ingredients to a shaker filled with ice, shake
sharply, and strain into a frosted martini glass. Garnish
with the lemon zest.

2 oz. Cytryonowka vodka

1 oz. lemon juice

1 oz. Cointreau

a dash of simple syrup

lemon zest, to garnish

french martini

2 oz. vodka

a large dash of Chambord or crème de mure

4 oz. fresh pineapple juice

This martini is great for parties since it is light
and creamy, and simple to make in bulk. Shake
this one hard when preparing it and you will be
rewarded with a thick white froth on the surface
of the drink.

Add all the ingredients to a shaker filled with ice, shake
sharply and strain into a frosted martini glass.

classic cosmopolitan

2 oz. lemon vodka
1 oz. triple sec
1 oz. lime juice
2 oz. cranberry juice

The TV program, *Sex and the City*, made this drink popular; its great taste has ensured it stays that way.

Add all the ingredients to a shaker filled with ice, shake sharply, and strain into a frosted martini glass.

ginger cosmopolitan

2 oz. lemon vodka
1 oz. triple sec
1 oz. fresh lime juice
2 oz. cranberry juice
2 thin ginger slices
flaming orange zest, to garnish

The mix of flaming orange zest, ginger, lime juice, and lemon vodka gives this drink an incredible depth of taste.

Add all the ingredients to a shaker filled with ice, shake sharply, and strain into a frosted martini glass. Garnish with a flaming orange zest.

harvey wallbanger

The story goes that Harvey, a Californian surfer who had performed particularly badly in an important contest, visited his local bar to drown his sorrows. He ordered his usual screwdriver—only to decide that it wasn't strong enough for what he had in mind. Scanning the bar for something to boost his drink, his eyes fell on a Galliano bottle, a shot of which was then added to his drink as a float.

2 oz. vodka
½ oz. Galliano
fresh orange juice, to top up
orange slice, to garnish

Build the ingredients over ice into a highball glass, stir, and serve with an orange slice.

sea breeze

2 oz. vodka
5 oz. cranberry juice
2 oz. fresh grapefruit juice
lime wedge, to garnish

The cranberry juice lends a light, fruity, refreshing quality and combines with the bitter grapefruit juice, making it very popular with people who don't really enjoy the taste of alcohol.

Pour the vodka into a highball glass filled with ice. Fill the glass three-quarter full with cranberry juice, and top with fresh grapefruit juice. Garnish with a lime wedge and serve with a straw.

gin

french 75

Named after the big artillery gun that terrorized the Germans during the First World War, rattling off rounds at a rate of 30 per minute. The popular variation on this drink was to mix cognac with the champagne, which would make sense since they were fighting in France!

Shake the gin, lemon juice, and simple syrup with ice and strain into a champagne flute. Top with champagne and garnish with a long strip of lemon zest.

1 oz. gin
2 teaspoons fresh lemon juice
1 teaspoon simple syrup
champagne, to top up
lemon zest, to garnish

gin gimlet

2 oz. gin
1 oz. lime cordial

A great "litmus" test for a bartender's capability—too much lime and the drink turns sickly, not enough and the drink is too strong. This one needs to be shaken hard to ensure a sharp freezing zestiness.

Add the gin and cordial to a shaker filled with ice. Shake very sharply and strain into a frosted martini glass.

negroni

The Negroni packs a powerful punch but still makes an elegant aperitif. For a drier variation, add a little more dry gin, but if a fruitier cocktail is more to your taste, wipe some orange zest around the top of the glass and add some to the drink.

1 oz. Campari
1 oz. sweet vermouth
1 oz. gin
orange zest, to garnish

Build all the ingredients into a rocks glass filled with ice, garnish with orange zest, and stir.

cowboy hoof

12 mint leaves, plus 1 to garnish
2 teaspoons simple syrup
2 oz. gin

The color of this drink alone is worth the effort. Pay attention when straining the mixture since bits of mint sticking to the teeth are never attractive!

Shake all the ingredients in a shaker filled with ice and strain through a fine mesh strainer into a frosted martini glass. Garnish with a sprig of fresh mint.

tequila

classic margarita

Beware, there are young pretenders out there who do not treat this cocktail with the respect it deserves. Margarita mixes, too much ice, and sweetened, concentrated lime juice instead of fresh juice, all contribute to an unacceptable cocktail. Don't let your margaritas be tarred by the same brush!

Shake all the ingredients sharply with cracked ice, then strain into a frosted margarita glass rimmed with salt.

2 oz. gold tequila
1 oz. triple sec or Cointreau
juice of ½ lime
salt, for the glass

triple gold margarita

Layered with a float of Goldschlager, the Triple Gold Margarita will bring a touch of splendor to any party. Laced with real 24-carat gold pieces, Goldschlager is a cinnamon-flavored liqueur that adds to the depth of taste of the cocktail.

Add all the ingredients except the Goldschlager to a shaker filled with ice. Shake sharply and strain into a frosted margarita glass. Float the Goldschlager onto the surface of the mixture, and serve.

2 oz. gold tequila
2 teaspoons Cointreau
2 teaspoons Grand Marnier
1 oz. fresh lime juice
½ oz. Goldschlager

tequila slammer

The Tequila Slammer is the ultimate machismo drink, and one that needs to be handled with care. This one is more likely to be imbibed for the sensation rather than the taste.

Pour both the tequila and the chilled champagne into an old-fashioned glass with a heavy bottom. Hold a napkin over the glass to seal the liquid inside. Sharply slam the glass down onto a stable surface, and drink in one go as the drink is fizzing.

2 oz. gold tequila
2 oz. chilled champagne

berry margarita

2 oz. gold tequila
½ oz. triple sec
½ oz. fresh lime juice
a dash of crème de mure
berries of your choice, plus extra to garnish

Anything from strawberries or cranberries, to blueberries or raspberries can be used in this recipe. Choose your own combination of seasonal berries for subtle variations.

Add all the ingredients to a blender. Add two scoops of crushed ice and blend for 20 seconds. Pour into a margarita coupette and garnish with berries.

submarine

Forget those age-old constraints of hard liquor and chaser standing alone. Opt instead for the Submarine and allow the tequila to seep gently from under its upturned shot glass and mingle with the beer before it hits the palate.

Pour the tequila into a shot glass. Holding the beer glass upside down, place the shot glass in it, so that it touches the bottom of the beer glass. Turn the beer glass the right way up so that the shot glass is upside down inside it, but the tequila is still inside the shot glass. Gently fill the beer glass with the beer. Serve.

2 oz. gold tequila
bottle Mexican beer (such as Sol)

los tres amigos

Lick, sip, suck—and enjoy!

Hold the lime wedge between the thumb and index finger. Pour the tequila into a shot glass and place the glass in the fleshy part of your hand between the same thumb and finger. Place the salt on the top of your hand next to the shot glass. In this order: lick the salt, shoot the tequila, and suck on the lime.

lime wedge
2 oz. gold tequila
a pinch of salt

rum &
caçhaca

jamaican breeze

The Jamaican Breeze is testament to Jamaican rum's ability to hold its own when mixed with a selection of flavors.

Pound the fresh ginger and rum together in the bottom of a shaker using a barspoon or muddler, then add ice and the remaining ingredients. Shake, and strain into a highball glass filled with ice.

2 thin fresh ginger slices

2 oz. white rum

3 oz. cranberry juice

3 oz. fresh pineapple juice

rum runner

1 oz. white rum

1 oz. dark rum

juice of ½ lime

½ oz. simple syrup

5 oz. fresh pineapple juice

The Rum Runner is a delicious example of rum's affinity with fresh juices as we've seen over the years in the classic Tiki cocktails and punches, made famous by Don the Beachcomber in the 1930s.

Shake all the ingredients sharply with ice in a shaker, then strain into a highball glass filled with crushed ice.

caipirinha

Cachaça, a liquor indigenous to Brazil, is distilled directly from the juice of sugar cane. The Caipirinha has made cachaça popular in many countries.

Cut the lime into eighths, squeeze, and place in an old-fashioned glass with the sugar, then pound well with a pestle. Fill the glass with crushed ice and add the cachaça. Stir vigorously and add simple syrup, to taste. Serve with two straws.

½ lime, quartered
heaped barspoon Demerara sugar
1 oz. cachaça
simple syrup, to taste

mojito

5 mint sprigs
2 oz. golden rum
a dash of fresh lime juice
2 dashes of simple syrup
club soda, to top up

Guaranteed to whisk you away to warmer, more tropical climes, the Mojito emerged in London over the summer of 1998 as the thinking man's refreshing tipple.

Put the mint in a highball glass, add the rum, lime juice and simple syrup, and muddle with a barspoon until the aroma of the mint is released. Add crushed ice and stir vigorously until the mixture and the mint is spread evenly. Top with club soda and stir again. Serve with straws.

original daiquiri

This classic cocktail was made famous at the El Floridita restaurant, Havana, early in the 20th century. Once you have found the perfect balance of light rum (traditionally Cuban), sharp citrus juice, and sweet simple syrup, stick to those measurements exactly.

Pour all the ingredients into an ice-filled shaker. Shake, and strain into a frosted martini glass.

2 oz. golden rum
½ oz. fresh lime juice
3 teaspoons simple syrup

orange daiquiri

The Orange Daiquiri substitutes the sweet Martinique rum called Creole Shrub for the Cuban rum of the Original Daiquiri, so uses a little less simple syrup to keep that delicate balance of sharp and sweet.

Pour all the ingredients into an ice-filled shaker. Shake, and strain into a frosted martini glass.

2 oz. Creole Shrub rum
¾ oz. fresh lime juice
1 teaspoon simple syrup

whiskey

premium manhattan

In a perfect world, every drink would be made out of the finest ingredients, but the cost means it's not always possible. Every so often though, it's worth splashing out and treating yourself and your guests.

Add all the ingredients to a mixing glass filled with ice, and stir gently with a barspoon. Strain into a frosted martini glass and garnish with orange zest.

2 oz. Knob Creek bourbon
1 oz. Vya dry vermouth
1 oz. Vya sweet vermouth
a dash of Angostura bitters
orange zest, to garnish

perfect manhattan

2 oz. rye whiskey
½ oz. sweet vermouth
½ oz. dry vermouth
a dash of Angostura bitters
orange zest, to garnish

"Perfect" does not refer to how well the drink is put together, it describes the perfect balance between sweet and dry. This manhattan is great served before supper in the depths of a cold winter.

Add the ingredients to a mixing glass filled with ice (first ensure all the ingredients are very cold) and stir the mixture until chilled. Strain into a frosted martini glass, add the garnish, and serve.

rusty nail

This one's purely for the colder months, when you are curled up in front of an open fire with a group of friends.

1 oz. Scotch
1 oz. Drambuie
orange zest, to garnish

Add both ingredients to a glass filled with ice and muddle with a barspoon. Garnish with orange zest.

sidecar

2 oz. brandy
1 oz. fresh lemon juice
1 oz. Cointreau
sugar, for the glass

The Sidecar, like many of the classic cocktails created in the 1920s, is attributed to the inventive genius of Harry McElhone, who founded Harry's New York Bar in Paris. It is said to have been created in honor of an eccentric military man who would roll up outside the bar in the sidecar of his chauffeur-driven motorcycle.

Shake all the ingredients together with ice and strain into a frosted martini glass rimmed with sugar.

champagne

rossini

A great variation on the Bellini, the Rossini is spiced up with a little Chambord and a dash of orange bitters—two of a bartender's favorite cocktail ingredients.

Add the purée, Chambord, and bitters to a champagne flute and top gently with champagne. Stir gently and serve.

½ oz. raspberry purée
1 teaspoon Chambord
2 dashes of orange bitters
champagne, to top up

mimosa

½ glass champagne
fresh orange juice, to top up

It is thought that Alfred Hitchcock invented this drink in an old San Francisco eatery called Jack's sometime in the 1940s, for a group of friends suffering from hangovers.

Pour the orange juice over half a flute-full of champagne and stir gently.

black velvet

I doubt if there is another drink in the world that looks more tempting and drinkable than a Black Velvet. Pour this drink gently into the glass to allow for the somewhat unpredictable nature of both the Guinness and the champagne.

½ glass Guinness
champagne, to top up

Half-fill a champagne flute with Guinness, gently top with champagne, and serve.

champagne cocktail

1 white sugar cube
2 dashes of Angostura bitters
1 oz. brandy
dry champagne, to top up

This cocktail has truly stood the test of time, being as popular now as when it was sipped by stars of the silver screen in the 1940s. It's a simple and delicious cocktail which epitomizes the elegance and sophistication of that era and still lends the same touch of urbanity (one hopes!) to those who drink it today.

Place the sugar cube in a champagne flute and moisten with Angostura bitters. Add the brandy, stir, then gently pour in the champagne and serve.

kir royale

After a shaky start, the Kir Royale is now the epitome of chic sophistication. It started life as the Kir (a variation using acidic white wine instead of champagne) and was labeled *rince cochon* (pig rinse!). Luckily, the wine became less sharp and the drink adopted a more appropriate mantle!

a dash of crème de cassis

champagne, to top up

Add a small dash of crème de cassis to a champagne flute and gently top with champagne. Stir gently and serve.

champagne julep

5 mint sprigs, plus 1 to garnish

2 barspoons sugar

a dash of simple syrup

a dash of lime juice

champagne, to top up

This cocktail works with all types of champagne or sparkling wine. If you have a bottle of bubbly that has been open for a while and lost a bit of its fizz, don't worry, the sugar in the recipe will revitalize it.

Muddle the mint, simple syrup, and lime juice together in a highball glass. Add crushed ice and the champagne (gently), and stir. Garnish with a mint sprig and serve.

non-alcoholic

cranberry cooler

It's so simple, I defy anyone not to admit that this drink, when served ice cold and in the right proportions, is the only thing that almost beats a lemonade made just right!

soda water
cranberry juice
1 lime wedge

Fill a tall highball glass with crushed ice. Pour in equal parts of soda water and then cranberry juice. Garnish with a squeeze of lime and serve with two straws.

st clement's

bitter lemon
fresh orange juice
lemon slice, to garnish

The name is taken from the English nursery rhyme "Oranges and Lemons said the bells of St. Clement's."

Build both ingredients (the bitter lemon first) in equal parts into a highball glass filled with ice. Stir gently, garnish with a lemon slice, and serve with two straws.

pussy foot

A surprising blend of bitter and sweet, tangy citrus
—most refreshing!

Shake the ingredients well with ice and strain into a
highball glass filled with ice.

3 oz. fresh cranberry juice
3 oz. fresh pineapple juice
3 oz. fresh orange juice
3 oz. fresh grapefruit juice
2 dashes of grenadine
a dash of fresh lemon juice

virgin mojito

6 mint sprigs, plus 1 to garnish
1 teaspoon superfine sugar
2 lime wedges
club soda, to top up
a dash of simple syrup

There's nothing in the manual that says cocktails
with no alcohol in them should be low maintenance
or one-dimensional. This one is a way of saying
thank you to anyone who has taken on the noble
role of designated driver for the night.

Muddle the mint, sugar, and lime in a highball glass filled
with ice. Fill with crushed ice, top with club soda and
muddle gently. Add simple syrup to taste, garnish with a
mint sprig, and serve with two straws.

index

conversion chart

Measures have been rounded up or down slightly
to make measuring easier. The key is to keep
ingredients in ratio.

Imperial	Metric
½ oz.	10–12.5 ml
1 oz. (single)	25 ml
2 oz. (double)	50 ml